Identity Cards

The Next Steps

WITHDRAWN

WITHDRAWN

Presented to Parliament
by the Secretary of State for the Home Department
by Command of Her Majesty
November 2003

Cm 6020

£4.75

Foreword

by the Home Secretary,
the Rt Hon David Blunkett MP

In this country we have a proud tradition of being a free and open society. Freedoms are not only embedded in our democracy, but in the very way we live our lives.

The world around us is changing very rapidly. Globalisation means movement of people on a scale unthinkable 50 years ago – nearly 90 million people a year arrive at UK ports. Technology has made life easier in so many ways, but has also opened up new crimes such as identity fraud that those involved in organised crime ruthlessly exploit. A secure form of personal identification would be a real benefit to individuals who want to establish their identity in day to day dealings with private and public sector organisations, including proving their entitlement to free public services. That is why the government has decided to build a base for a compulsory national identity cards scheme. We intend to proceed by incremental steps, building on existing widely held identity documents and requiring foreign nationals to obtain documents which are currently issued on a voluntary basis.

This follows a lengthy public consultation under Cabinet Office guidelines. I am immensely grateful to the many members of the public and organisations who contributed to the consultation. I have today published a separate paper which sets out the responses and the results of surveys and polling which demonstrated substantial commitment to some form of identity card, a term the public preferred to the term 'entitlement card'.

Identity cards will provide every person in this country with an easy and secure way of demonstrating their right to be here and of asserting their place in the community. With the proper safeguards on our privacy, the scheme will bring benefits to each of us as individuals but also provide mutual benefits to our society as a whole. Our liberties will be strengthened if our identity is protected from theft; if we are guaranteed access to the services to which we are entitled; and if our community is better protected from terrorists and organised criminals, and from those who seek to abuse the immigration rules and public services.

This Government was elected to modernise and ensure our country is equipped to face the challenges of the 21st century. Our proposal for a national identity cards scheme is about modernising our way of life, using technology so that we are all able to live more securely in the future and so building a stronger society.

DAVID BLUNKETT

Introduction

1. The combination of greater global mobility and advancing technology is making it increasingly difficult to protect and authenticate people's identity. As a result, we face growing threats to the security and prosperity of British citizens from illegal migration and working, organised crime and terrorism, identity theft & fraud and fraudulent access to public services, for example by illegal migrants who have no entitlement to them. That is why biometric passports are already being developed here, elsewhere in Europe and the USA.

2. The Government has decided to begin the process of introducing a national identity cards scheme as a key part of a comprehensive strategy to contain these threats and ensure more reliable means of authenticating people's identity. In the light of these threats and other international developments which are driving up the standards required to prove identity, doing nothing is not a option. Our proposals are designed to protect, not erode, civil liberties, by protecting people's true identity against fraud and by enabling them to prove their identity more easily without unnecessary intrusion by State or private interests.

3. We will proceed in two stages:

    FIRST STAGE

    *   Once the Office of Government Commerce (OGC) has confirmed that the programme is ready to proceed,[1] we will publish draft legislation to enable the scheme to be introduced and pave the way for the establishment of more reliable means of proving people's identity. This will include:

    (i)   establishing a National Identity Register;
    (ii) proceeding towards more secure passports and driving licences based on biometric technology – with personalised, specific identifiers;
    (iii) for those who do not need a passport or driving licence and choose to take it up, making available a voluntary plain identity card. This would not, of course, become compulsory (or be mandatory for access to services) until the appropriate further Parliamentary decision – see below;

---

1   By means of an OGC Gateway 0 review.

(iv) introducing mandatory biometric identity documents for foreign nationals coming to stay in the UK for longer than 3 months. For nationals from countries in the European Economic Area (EEA) this will be done in a way which is fully compatible with European law.[2]

- The costs of these steps and all start-up costs, will be met from charging or from existing departmental budgets.
- The introduction of plain identity cards on a phased basis will, on current plans, start from 2007/8 and, together with the incremental roll-out of biometric passports and perhaps eventually driving licences, might be expected to cover 80% of the economically active population within five years.
- There will be close work across Government to develop effective technology particularly on biometrics and to introduce systems to ensure that biometric data can be collected, stored and used effectively. This will include a 6 month biometric pilot which will shortly be run by the UK Passport Service to test the recording of face, iris and fingerprint biometric information.

SECOND STAGE

If the conditions were right, this first stage phased roll-out could then be followed by a move to a compulsory card scheme in which it would be compulsory to have a card – though not to carry one – and to produce a card to access public services in ways defined by those services. In the case of those services for which the devolved administrations have responsibility, decisions on production of a card to access those services would be a matter for them.

The move to compulsion would require full debate and a vote in both houses of Parliament. Clearly the Government would only take this step after a rigorous evaluation of the first stage, when it was confident that everything was in place to enable the scheme to work successfully, that its benefits outweighed any costs and risks and that it was fully affordable within future agreed spending plans. In particular, we would want to be confident that:

- roll out during the first phase has already delivered significant coverage of the population;
- there is clear public acceptance for the principle of a compulsory ID card which would be used to access free public services. This would already have included a scheme of charges based on cost recovery and subsidy for those on low incomes;

---

2 EEA nationals would obtain biometric identity documents as part of the registration process which is compatible with existing EU law and with the draft Directive on Free Movement of Persons.

- use of the card for access to free public services would not prevent people without cards from accessing emergency services, and those on low incomes and other vulnerable groups would not be disadvantaged;
- the scheme would make a further significant difference to tackling fraudulent access to free public services, and to tackling illegal working at an acceptable compliance cost to business;

and

- the technology is working and public services have implemented the technology and business changes necessary to take full advantage of the scheme.

Why do we need an identity cards scheme?

4.   The UK has traditionally depended on strong external borders but in today's changing world the lack of internal immigration controls is a major contributor to the 'pull factor' which draws people here illegally. Those who arrive and work illegally are often earning less than the minimum wage. This creates tensions in the resident community, especially with those on low incomes, and fosters fears among established minority ethnic groups that their acceptance may be undermined. Employers and service providers often have great difficulty in checking whether people are entitled to work or to access services because of the plethora of documents which they need to check. This creates pressure on already hard-pressed public services and small businesses and makes enforcement against unscrupulous employers difficult.

5.   Today legal migrants contribute both to the UK economy (an estimated net fiscal contribution of £2.5 billion pa) and to our public services, for instance filling vital posts in the NHS. We need to continue to encourage people to come to the UK legitimately to work. At the same time, management of overall migration, including illegal migration must be effective in order to reassure the resident population in the UK.

6.   The identity cards scheme will be an inclusive scheme, designed to cover everyone who has the right to be here. It will show that everyone belongs to our society whether they were born here, have chosen to make their home here or are just staying for a while to study or work. It will help people prove their identity to access services such as free health treatment or benefits and give everyone confidence that legal migration will not result in increased fraudulent use of hard-pressed public services. If our communities have confidence in our immigration controls, they will be more welcoming of new arrivals, helping to promote a more cohesive society.

7. Terrorists use false and multiple identities to help undertake and finance their activities in the UK and abroad. False and multiple identities are also essential 'tools of the trade' for organised crime to facilitate money laundering and also other crimes which cause the most misery in our communities such as drugs misuse and drug-related crimes, people-trafficking, prostitution and people working illegally in unsafe and overcrowded conditions. Disrupting these activities is a key priority. The development of unique identifiers linked to the National Identity Register will help tackle these problems and protect our communities. The card is a simple and easy way of achieving this in a manner that is beneficial to the individual as well as to society as a whole.

8. Identity fraud costs the economy at least £1.3 billion every year. Individuals pay for this in general through higher charges for financial services. There can also be a heavy personal cost in putting right credit ratings and in extreme cases parents suffering the trauma of having a deceased child's identity stolen. While there are some cases of straightforward theft of a person's identity, identity fraud is rarely committed for its own sake, rather it is an enabler for other offences such as money laundering. It has been estimated that false identities are used to launder around £390m every year. A cards scheme will help by providing a secure means to verify identity either in person or where the applicant is not present but gives consent, by organisations checking with the National Identity Register. Above all it prevents multiple identities being used for such purposes.

9. Across public services there are already many situations in which statutory services require an individual to produce proof of identity, for example, in claiming benefits, in taking up a place in Higher Education, applying for a student loan, or in applying for social housing. An identity card which was a recognised Government-confirmed proof of identity, would mean that an individual would not need to provide many different cards or pieces of paper, and would combat impersonation and identity fraud. Offering an identity card at a much reduced cost for those on low incomes and the elderly will give them a means of proving their identity that many others take for granted. As well as providing a more convenient way for those entitled to services to access them, an identity card will also help to prevent unauthorised access to services. An example would be claims to free non-emergency NHS treatment by people whose immigration status does not entitle them to this treatment. By giving a clear indication that a person is not entitled to free treatment, a card scheme will help combat health tourism. A card would not be mandatory for verification of entitlement to services in the voluntary phase until the appropriate further Parliamentary decision on a move to compulsion.

How will the scheme benefit individuals?

10.   As well as the benefits to the country as a whole, for the individual, identity cards will:

    (i)   help them establish their identity and right to access services in a simple, easy and convenient way, making it faster to prove their identity for public or private transactions including electronic services;

    (ii) potentially reduce time spent queuing at ports by using the card at fast track immigration checking facilities;

    (iii) enable them to assert their identity and that they belong here;

    (iv) protect them from identity fraud;

    (v) help to increase confidence in the security and integrity of our immigration controls, leading to a more cohesive society.

What was learned from the consultation exercise?

11.   Individual responses, sample surveys, and polling results have demonstrated substantial support for an identity card. Of the 5,000 people and organisations who responded formally to the consultation, 4,200 expressed a view. Over 60% of these were in favour. We also received over 5,000 e-mails from an organised opposition campaign. Over 96% of these were opposed.

12.   We commissioned wider research which involved both focus groups and polling which confirmed, as independent polling has done, 80% of the general public were in favour of identity cards, including comparable levels of support among the four main minority ethnic groupings. Similar results across all geographic and socio-economic groups emerged from the detailed interviews with members of the public.

13.   The consultation demonstrated that the public prefer the term "identity card" to "entitlement card" and we accept their judgement.

How will the Government proceed?

14.   We recognise the size of the step we are proposing and we will therefore proceed incrementally. Experience shows that the "big bang" approach is not the way to introduce a complex programme involving new technology and major business change. We have always intended, as we set out in the consultation document published in July 2002, that any scheme would

have to be based on the existing processes for issuing passports and driving licences and, as such, would be incremental in its approach.

15. A National Identity Register of basic personal information will be created as part of the scheme. It will be built from scratch as people are issued with identity cards and not rely solely on other sources of data which may have historical or other errors. However, before an entry is confirmed, it will be checked against other databases such as passports, driving licences and immigration records. The Register will also link each individual's record to a biometric that is unique to that person. The National Identity Register will therefore be a single highly reliable record of a person's identity and will be built using best practice in countering identity fraud. People will have confidence that their personal information will be held securely and cannot be stolen or abused by others.

WHAT IS BIOMETRIC INFORMATION?

A unique identifying physical characteristic. Examples include facial recognition, iris patterns and fingerprints. Recording biometric information at local, convenient access points will help to ensure that a person's identity record is associated with information unique to that person. The biometric information can be stored on a chip on the card and on the National Identity Register. The uniqueness of biometric information will help prevent people's identities being stolen and also will securely confirm a person's identity when a card is checked.

16. A high level of coverage of the population will be achieved over time by:

(i) requiring foreign nationals coming here for more than 3 months, to obtain a card in the form of a more secure residence permit than that which is currently available on a voluntary basis;

(ii) linking more secure passports and perhaps eventually driving licences to the scheme on a compulsory basis so that they will be acceptable forms of identity card. By linking the card scheme to widely held identity documents most people will get a card conveniently and automatically as they renew an existing document;

(iii) introducing a voluntary plain identity card available for those who do not need a passport or driving licence and who choose to take it up. As already discussed, this would not become compulsory (or be mandatory for access to services) until the appropriate further Parliamentary decision;

(iv) working closely with business – particularly small business – trade unions and others to design the scheme to maximise the benefits and minimise the compliance costs to law-abiding businesses and to develop an effective enforcement system that will deal with illegal workers and the minority of businesses that deliberately flout the law. In the first stage it will not be a requirement to possess a card in order to work or obtain a National Insurance number;

(v)   encouraging private sector organisations to make use of the identity cards scheme to make appropriate checks on identity for example when opening bank accounts. In addition, it will be important to investigate the potential benefits to the private sector of more secure systems for establishing identity and the extent to which the private sector might be willing to contribute financially;

(vi)   working with the NHS and other public services to maximise the benefits of a card and minimise the compliance costs.

17.   No one would ever be refused medical treatment in an emergency or emergency social security benefits nor would vulnerable groups be refused critical services such as access to hostels or refuges (where of course they would be assisted to acquire acceptable identification) because they were unable to produce an identity card. The cards scheme will be designed to help people access services, particularly foreign nationals whose identity documents might be unfamiliar. While if we proceeded to stage two of our proposals, it would eventually become compulsory for everyone to have an identity card, it would not be compulsory to carry an identity card. At this stage, organisations would be able to specify when a card needed to be produced to access their services, subject to approval where necessary by Parliament.

How much will this cost?

18.   Most people will join the scheme when they apply for or renew their driving licence or passport for which charges are already levied. The minimum charge to obtain a 10 year passport is £42; from March 2004, the full cost of obtaining an initial 10 year driving licence will be £38. In practice the cost that many people currently pay for these documents is around £8-£10 higher when taking account of the cost of photographs and services which check that forms have been completed correctly and the right documentation enclosed. Neither of these costs would be incurred in a national identity cards scheme. It is clear that people are prepared to pay for a long-lasting document which increases the convenience to them of proving their correct identity. Recent research confirms that the majority of people would be willing to pay something for an identity card which has individual and social benefits. Of course with the development of biometric documentation, the cost would be incurred in any event but without the transparency which is now being presented in terms of the use of such identifiers for the national identity cards scheme.

19. We recognise that paying for anything places a burden on the individual and therefore we must minimise the cost and inconvenience. If we did not implement a wider scheme but concentrated purely on implementing more secure passports and driving licences including biometrics, initial estimates suggest that the 10 year cost of passports would rise to around £73 and driving licences to around £69.

20. Under the national identity cards scheme, our best estimate at this stage is that:

   (i) a 10 year plain identity card would cost most people in the order of £35;

   (ii) a combined passport/identity card would cost £77, and a combined driving licence/identity card would cost £73 (though holders of both documents would only pay the full cost for the first one they renewed). In other words, around £4 more per person spread across 10 years than if we did not implement the wider scheme and simply included biometrics on existing documents.

   This would fund free cards for all 16 year olds and a reduced charge of £10 for those on low incomes. We are looking at how those who have been in retirement for some time could obtain a lifelong card, requiring no further payment and are also looking at whether plain identity cards could be paid for by installments.

21. For very frail and elderly citizens it would be possible to issue a non-biometric card (for instance those with severe learning disabilities who are in residential care or those over 80).

22. These cost estimates include a contingency factor.

How will people's privacy be protected?

23. The legislation will allow the cards scheme to be used by any service – public or private – to establish identity with the consent of the card-holder, but with strict limits on the information available. Only Parliament would be able to change the statutory purposes of the scheme or the information which could be held by the scheme.

24. Data held on the National Identity Register will be basic identity information – such as name, address, date of birth, gender, immigration status and a confirmed biometric – and this will be set out in statute. Organisations using the National Register to verify identity will not be able to get to other personal information, for instance health or tax records, via the Register.

25. The police and other organisations will not have routine access to data stored on the National Identity Register. However there are strong arguments for giving them such access to help fight serious crime and terrorism. Such access will be set out in statute and there will be independent oversight of the arrangements as there is at the present time. There will be no new power for the police to stop someone and demand to see their card.

Next steps

26. The Government is determined to ensure that the development of a national identity cards scheme is managed to the highest standards, and that the major business change and IT challenges which we face are dealt with effectively. A Programme Board is being established chaired by the Home Office to co-ordinate and drive forward the different elements of the Government strategy. Progress at every stage will be monitored and reviewed as further decisions are taken during the implementation. Before decisions are taken on implementation, there will be an intensive phase of feasibility assessment and prototyping so that decision making is soundly based and risks in the programme are kept to a minimum.

27. Once the Office of Government Commerce has confirmed that the programme is ready to proceed, by means of an OGC Gateway 0 review, we will publish draft legislation to enable the scheme to be introduced.

28. We continue to welcome the views of the public, business, commerce, unions and others and these can be sent to *(IdentityCards@homeoffice.gsi.gov.uk)*.

Printed in the UK for The Stationery Office Limited
on behalf of the Controller of Her Majesty's Stationery Office
ID 159495 11/03 077240